Seeing what real estate investing has done in my own life and the lives of others, Roger's book will assist any newcomers into the arena! Take note, there are great things to learn here!

—RAIYAN RAB
Founder/Owner, Numarix Brokerage

As an investor, house flipper, and owner of numerous fix-and-holds, Roger Becker's timely book on funding solutions speaks to the challenges with funding I have faced. His innovative and creative ideas have allowed me to expand my business through his eye-opening funding solutions.

—THOMAS PETRILLO
Results Coach/Business Res

T0145676

When I was first exploring the idea of going out on my own, Roger gave me the courage and confidence that I could do it. I remember one conversation in our infancy of starting BZ Hospitality together where Roger specifically said, "Jayson, you can do this, you have the experience and skills to be successful." Sometimes in life you need someone to inspire you to take a giant leap and Roger has often been that guiding force for our company; for that I am truly grateful.

—JAYSON ZIMMER

Co-Founder, BZ Hospitality

We all learn something new every day and simplicity helps get us there. Roger breaks down the complex step by step as he describes the art of borrowing money while simplifying the process. If you've thought about borrowing, buying and flipping homes, Roger's book will provide the inspiration and know-how to get you started. I highly recommend it.

—RORY MCCREESH

President, Duce Construction Corp

If you're interested in flipping houses or simply learning how to bootstrap your way to success, do yourself a favor and read *The Funding Solution.* You'll be inspired—and impressed—by Roger Becker's personal story, which he uses to encourage readers to pursue their own dreams. Becker shares what he has learned from doing over forty-five house flips to provide an easy-to-understand blueprint for putting together creative real estate deals that can help you (and your future partners) achieve financial independence.

—ROBERT O'LEARY
Regional Vice President, Choice Hotels

A first-class primer on investing in "flips" from a guy with real-world experience. An honest look at what it takes to be successful in the fascinating world of real estate investing in easy bite-sized pieces that is sure to fill even the healthiest investment appetite. Bon appétit!

—TODD HUNNICUTT
CEO, Real Internet Sales

You won't find another book on house flipping that is so honest and transparent about mistakes made, and so clear about how to avoid them. Roger's simple approach and flip calculator tool are priceless assets for today's new house flipper—a must-read!

—DREW MOORE
CEO, Suited

In *The Funding Solution,* Roger Becker demystifies the house flip process! Starting with identifying the "why" and educating in easy-to-understand terms the steps involved, he spurs you to go for it and create the life you always dreamed of. With stories from his and his wife Stacey's own adventures, the book is engaging and full of attainable action steps. Roger provides resources, tools, and suggestions that are invaluable to the house flip endeavor. Truly, reading this book makes me feel equipped and eager to "roll up my sleeves, get out there, and change my future *now*!"

—SIMONA NEDELISKY
Aspiring Entrepreneur, Gresham, OR

THE
FUNDING
SOLUTION

THE FUNDING SOLUTION

A GUIDE TO HARD MONEY LOANS AND BUILDING WEALTH THROUGH CREATIVE LENDING

ROGER BECKER

Published by Advantage, Charleston, South Carolina.
Member of Advantage Media Group.

ADVANTAGE is a registered trademark, and the Advantage colophon is a trademark of Advantage Media Group, Inc.

Printed in the United States of America.

10 9 8 7 6 5 4 3 2 1

ISBN: 978-1-64225-352-8
LCCN: 2021919671

Cover design by Carly Blake.
Layout design by Mary Hamilton.

This publication is designed to provide accurate and authoritative information in regard to the subject matter covered. It is sold with the understanding that the publisher is not engaged in rendering legal, accounting, or other professional services. If legal advice or other expert assistance is required, the services of a competent professional person should be sought.

Advantage Media Group is proud to be a part of the Tree Neutral® program. Tree Neutral offsets the number of trees consumed in the production and printing of this book by taking proactive steps such as planting trees in direct proportion to the number of trees used to print books. To learn more about Tree Neutral, please visit **www.treeneutral.com**.

Advantage Media Group is a publisher of business, self-improvement, and professional development books and online learning. We help entrepreneurs, business leaders, and professionals share their Stories, Passion, and Knowledge to help others Learn & Grow. Do you have a manuscript or book idea that you would like us to consider for publishing? Please visit **advantagefamily.com** or call **1.866.775.1696**.

I'd like to dedicate this book to my wife Stacey.

From the time we worked together at the ages of nineteen and twenty, selling door-to-door in blistering summer weather, and then trying to encourage and coax other lackadaisical teenagers to do the same; to starting one fast food restaurant and then crazily a second one together; always with late, late hours helping crunch numbers and get into the finer details. I wouldn't be here without you!

*Always a pillar I can lean on, you always have believed we could accomplish our dreams together; here's to believing with all your heart—
no matter what, never, ever give up!*

CONTENTS

FOREWORD

Roger is the quintessential entrepreneur, and look no further than his own business as the case study for the tools he provides in this book.

I've watched Roger grow his business exponentially in just a handful of years, paving a path of success free from constraints or limitations on the types of projects he's willing to take on, allowing for opportunities with diversity, and building a portfolio of project experience that rivals those of seasoned developers and general contractors.

He saw opportunity when most would rather swim in a glass half empty for weeks after being let go from a company. Instead, Roger dove head first into a brand new career, finding opportunity in our insane real estate market, one that supports taking on projects that may be outside one's wheelhouse, projects where the downside risk is career-ending.

From house flipper to successful builder/developer with a diverse and growing portfolio of projects, Roger has managed to do in five years what many spend their careers trying to achieve. More importantly, he has built a portfolio that will help him weather any market the real estate roller coaster brings us next.

There's no *Development for Dummies* or *Cliffs Notes* when it comes to this business, and no two projects are *ever* the same.

Roger offers honest, detailed experiences invaluable to anyone new to the real estate game. More important is to understand that *his* experiences aren't going to be *your* experiences, so knowledge is key in a process with thousands of moving parts, and too many outside influences that consistently affect your project from start to finish.

Beyond the wealth of detailed info he provides, there's a bigger picture that I truly believe he offers, and what I believe are some of the roots to his success:

Lose the fear. Find the positives, as every project has TONS of negatives. Make decisions knowing both, be patient, and ask questions—don't be afraid and don't pretend to know more than you really do (it's obvious, trust me). No question is a dumb question in this biz.

Network. Surround yourself and work with those you trust. From a "Daddy Warbucks" to designers/engineers, having reliable contacts can make or break a project.

Roll with the Punches. Life deals us cards, so learn to play with them as Roger addresses. If this were easy, everyone would be doing it. Plenty try, few succeed, most think that the pretty new truck with the sticker on the side makes you a successful contractor in a market like this. The better option, as Roger says: "Roll up your sleeves, get out there, and change your future *now!*"

—CHRIS MCDONALD

Founder/Owner, Developing Services Inc.

INTRODUCTION

FIRST FLIP

$50,000 IN THE BANK

In 2016, I walked into the fourplex unit that would become my first house flip; all I saw was absolute shambles. Under foreclosure, the inside was trashed with disgusting carpets, cracks in the tile floor, hand-drawn paintings on the walls, garbage, and boxes of neglected stuff in every room. There were even hair trimmings in the master bedroom matted into the floor—gross! It certainly wasn't much to look at, and the smell wasn't great either.

I also saw an excellent investment for this area of

the Pacific Northwest with a modest $79,000 price tag. I saw a bright, polished future with granite tile countertops, new appliances, freshly painted walls, and planted gardens. I used $10,000 of personal savings to secure the loan and did most of the work with my wife, Stacey, and friend Brad. Hard costs for the work totaled $8,512, so our total cash investment was $18,512. I put the property up for sale for $139,000, and it sold for $155,100 (the final sale totaled $155,207.26 with closing costs and added interest) after a battle between two buyers. I was hooked.

The gross profit from the sale was $67,695, net $49,183. With that kind of return on investment, I paid off debts and started planning a better future for my family. Best of all, I could invest in another project! As the old saying goes, "Success breeds success!"

Over the next four years, we kept investing and flipping. By the end of 2020, I had completed forty-five house flips with help from partners and numerous lenders. I even started two companies that do house flips and new construction with both hard-money and private lending. But that didn't come easily or fear-lessly. I had so much to learn.

In the beginning, I didn't exactly have $79,000 lying around for that first flip. Where would the money come from? What if banks turned up their noses at a novice? What lending options did I have? Was hard money a good option? What about private lending—where could we find an investor who trusted us, and vice versa?

Walking into that first decrepit unit, I knew I could transform it. I trusted my vision and the team's abilities to flip the place on a shoestring budget. The real fear came with the steps leading up to purchasing the property and future investments. I had wanted to try this kind of real estate investment for years but, like many people, feared the unknown. I assumed I would borrow money through the traditional bank process and came across all kinds of deals over the years, distressed houses and foreclosures—but never had the wherewithal or courage to jump on them.

> **I TRUSTED MY VISION AND THE TEAM'S ABILITIES TO FLIP THE PLACE ON A SHOE-STRING BUDGET.**

I didn't understand the benefit of partnerships or having more than one lender. I didn't know the difference between a hard-money lender and a private-money lender. I had no idea where to get a big-money lender or that knocking down doors (and having patience) would be so crucial. I didn't know anything, really. It wasn't until a friend recommended a lender for that first flip that I gained the know-how and courage to take the leap!

Learning about that first lender helped me take my first steps. Discovering a lender who would secure a loan with less money down encouraged me to go after that first opportunity. Since then, I've learned about and am open to different lending opportunities; I have worked with small and significant investments. I learned a ton and am able and eager to share what I learned with you. I encourage you to go after similar opportunities to provide a better future for you and your family.

If you've been too nervous about taking the first step in becoming an investor or business owner, this book is for you. I was an average guy with no experience when I got started. After a long hospitality sales career, I came to the crossroads that helped push me into the life I now love. This book will give you the tools to take those first steps.

The following chapters will:

- demystify the lending process and show you that being entrepreneurial means knocking down doors;

- explain the importance of having more than one lender (especially in a volatile market like we experienced during the COVID-19 pandemic);

- discuss ways to avoid or handle things that can go wrong;

- provide tips on how to conduct your first investment and how to progress into your second, third, and beyond; and

- arm you with the tools you need to build capital through real estate investments and start your own business.

RESOURCES TO GET YOU STARTED

1. QR: There are QR codes at the end of each chapter directing you to videos reviewing the finances on a specific flip project to give you an idea of what is possible for you.

2. Lenders: I include a comprehensive list of lenders at the end of this book you can use right away.

3. Website: www.thefundingsolutionbook.com has additional and new resources. I want this handbook to be a springboard for readers, providing helpful tools to get you going and to help improve your game.

My goal is that by the end of this book, you will have

the knowledge and confidence to achieve goals that allow you to make a significant difference in your family's life and the lives of others!

CHAPTER ONE

WHY INVEST

WHAT'S YOUR NORTH STAR?

 For that first flip project, I partnered with my friend Brad Rohr. Seeing our hard work pay off was euphoric, so Brad and I searched for the next deal almost immediately.

Within just a few weeks, we were knee deep in flipping an old row house we bought out of foreclosure. With this mostly cosmetic upgrade, we busied ourselves painting, replacing carpets, and installing new appliances. Our hard work paid off again, with the gross proceeds at closing a surprising $59,580.65.

For flip number three, we connected with a new-to-us lender we met through another house flipper. I couldn't believe how much I was learning about the benefit of partnerships and the variety of lending opportunities out there. I felt more and more excited about how straightforward the flipping business was. I purchased a property, fixed it up, and then sold it and went on to the next project. I loved this entire process.

During this time, I still worked full-time in sales for a hotel company. I daydreamed about making this new passion my only job but didn't have the nerve to make the leap to being 100 percent in business for myself flipping houses.

Then fate stepped in.

In April 2017, I returned from a spring break trip on a Monday morning to learn I had lost my job. While my family and I had vacationed, my company merged with another, making my position redundant. Within an hour of this big announcement, I was let go with a severance package. I could have been angry or, worse yet, dispirited. Instead, my wife and I took this opportunity (yes, I refer to this as an opportunity!) to sit down and really explore flipping houses as a real, full-time business option and primary source of income.

I decided to go for it, become an entrepreneur, start my own business, and let the cards fall where they may. I had owned a business before, but this was my first time starting from the beginning. A few years back, I had purchased a taco restaurant, Taco Del Mar, and ultimately ran two of them (more on that later!).

The experience I had from the Taco Del Mar business gave me the confidence to start a construction company with a partner. That said, while I did have business ownership experience, creating a completely new company is very different from taking over an established one. We did it and began flipping houses before expanding to new construction, remodeling, and renovations.

Early on, we realized we needed a "why" to make this work. I found many. My first "why" was to support my family and free up more time to spend with them. My second "why" was something that I had begun to care deeply about: the value of "build beautiful." When you are a flipper, you sometimes get focused solely on the dollars—some flippers do what we call "slapping lipstick on a pig." As we moved forward, I can honestly say that we committed never to have this approach for our team and business. No cutting corners. Our goal was to go above and beyond remodeling homes, to not just make them new again, but truly to "build beautiful." We didn't want to create a simple flip business focused on making a quick buck. We wanted to start a company (an adventure!) and make a lasting, beautiful impact with every project we did.

In 2019, we rebranded, renaming the company Vibe Construction, and focused our work on projects that elevated and gave a distinctly "good vibe" to anyone who bought one of our homes. Our hard work and positioning paid off; my wife and I are well on our way to paying off our home, vehicles, and even investing in our first hotel!

I ENCOURAGE YOU TO CONSIDER YOUR WHYS; LET YOUR WHYS COME FROM THE HEART.

What's your big why? Do you want flexibility with your time and lifestyle? Do you want financial freedom? From taking care of an aging parent to paying off a student loan, there is a long list of what you can do with investment funds.

I encourage you to consider your whys; let your whys come from the heart.

Hundreds of years ago, explorers guided their vessels across unknown expanses, vast oceans, to reach never-before-explored destinations. They hoped to find new, unconquered lands never seen. The stars charted their journeys. Similarly, slaves escaping slavery in the South followed the North Star along the Underground Railroad to find freedom.

As you embark on your journey, explore alternate means of living your dreams, supporting your family, and finding incredible financial freedom. You may be charting an unknown course, but having a North Star keeps you on track.

Before you begin, examine why this is important to you. Write all your whys down in black and white to refer back to on days when you doubt yourself. Whether you've taken a giant leap or are currently in a job you want to leave, focus on your *why*; what's your core motivating factor? Why do you want more? Find that and hold onto it; let it be your North Star.

FIVE TIPS FOR FIRST-TIME FLIPPERS

What do I recommend to first-time flippers? From knowing where to look for a deal or where to start with lenders, here are some basic first steps all beginner flippers should keep in mind as they start.

TIP 1: LOOK FOR A SMALL DEAL FIRST

My first-ever property deal (not a house flip) was a piece of land in Alaska. Yes, you heard that correctly: Alaska! It was right after the 2008 recession, and I wanted to make a smart move with my savings, so I bought nine acres for only $6,000. By the time I got around to selling in 2010, I had managed to get a 50 percent return on it. The ROI was ideal, but the key was keeping the initial deal small.

Those kinds of deals are hard to find, but I couldn't borrow (and put 20 percent down) at the time, so I had to be persistent. My determination then still pays off today and will for you, too. Start *small* first; keep it modest out of the gate!

TIP 2: LOOK FOR DEALS NEARBY

Trust me when I tell you that keeping things close to home saves you a lot of time and hassle. I probably would have sold that land a lot sooner if it weren't so very far away. But that's just land—being close to your house flip is even more crucial. Our first flip was a mile away from my house. Traveling too far from your general vicinity for your early deals takes a toll on you. Even when you're not getting your hands dirty, you want to be nearby to check on contractors' progress. You can do deals farther away as you get a few under your belt, but stay *nearby* when you first get going.

TIP 3: EXPLORE MANY LENDERS TO BREAK DOWN BARRIERS TO BORROWING

Don't be afraid to shake the different lending trees that are out there. If you're like me, you've probably faced rejection from banks not loaning you money one time or another. It took time to realize that I may need to partner with something to land my first property deal. It took even longer to learn that my lending options were varied; hard money (attained via capital, not credit) and private money (secured via an individual or individuals, not a company) are both viable and attainable. I also learned I didn't need to go with a traditional bank loan, and having more than one lender is ideal. I learned that knocking down doors until I got what I needed would pay off. I even learned about owner financing, even more simplified, nonbank transactions out there waiting to be discovered.

I'll fully explore hard money, private lending, and owner financing, as well as why they're all great opportunities in chapters 2 through 4. Whether your credit score isn't great, or you simply don't want to be in debt to a bank, you will want to take notes in chapters 2 through 4.

TIP 4: DON'T BE AFRAID TO PARTNER UP

Consider getting a partner, especially for your first deal. It may be someone you haven't known long; you just want to be sure they are serious about the investment.

Remember, partnering on a house flip is different from partnering for a business or a franchise. With house flips, there's a beginning and an end. It's all conveniently short term. If it doesn't work out, or your partner isn't amazing, you can move on upon project completion. Most flips take place within a year, from beginning to end; your timeline is somewhat straightforward. And if it goes well, great! Now you can work together again.

Something to bear in mind is that family members tend to be more hesitant than others on that first deal— you may need to prove yourself before a relative or even a close friend will take that risk with you.

Don't let the fear of rejection give you reservations on fielding a partner in the first place. Having a partner allows you to overcome lots of fears. Your partner's different skill set is often complementary to yours, allowing you both to take on slightly different roles. This dynamic can help you run things efficiently, find quick solutions for challenges, and stay focused on what you both bring to the project.

TIP 5: RUB SHOULDERS WITH A LOCAL IN THE KNOW

If you can, try to talk to an area house flipper. You may not know one, so contact your local real estate offices to see if their agents work with flippers or are flippers themselves. (Savvy Realtors do a flip a year; one might be a perfect first partner. The agent's motivation will be to sell the house once finished.) Find and maximize opportunities like this to ask many questions and explore the whole process; they can help you with your first flip.

And don't forget the why. Making a better life for yourself and your family can always be a great guide! It has been for me.

Remember that first flip, the dingy fourplex unit where I made a $50,000 profit? Getting my check was a thrill like I had never experienced in my life!

When you turn that first profit and it's more than what you're making at another job, it is easy to keep that momentum and euphoric high in mind. It's impossible to forget! Getting that feeling repeatedly definitely motivates me.

BEFORE

AFTER

Know that a big check with your name on it is possible; this can happen for you too. Take that entrepreneurial leap of faith; step out and do a small project with a partner. There will be challenges and learning curves, but you will work through them. Then you go to close, and you see that check; that is an exhilarating moment. It's liberating. It boosts your self-confidence and opens up more doors. Flipping a house can be the avenue to a whole world of opportunities.

But first: How in the world can you afford it? Let's start by exploring why I'm such a fan of hard-money lending.

The before and after pictures to the left are of a house we flipped near Leavenworth, Washington; this video is the story about that flip.

CHAPTER TWO

HARD-MONEY LOANS

THE NUTS AND BOLTS

What are hard-money loans? Where did that name come from? Are they hard to get? Are they a bad way to invest, so hardly a good option? Maybe you thought hard-money loans are similar to payday lenders, with their usurious interest rates of 25 to 40 percent! I can tell you one thing; hard-money loans are not payday lender loans. Most hard-money lenders guard against interest rates going higher than 12 percent because of usury laws or regulations governing rates in different states.

Hard-money loans are a means of financing while eliminating many of the hurdles experienced with bank loans because hard-money loans come from private businesses or investors, not banks.

When exploring my first flip options, I definitely didn't want to put down 20 percent, the usual cost needed for a traditional loan. However, Brad and I had enough capital (10 percent combined) to offer our hard-money lender, Iron Bridge Lending. The other factor brought to the lender is that I would finance our improvements on the flip.

What Iron Bridge liked about the deal is how cheaply I could buy the unit; searching for and finding that great deal is part of the challenge here. They also liked that I planned to do the fix-up out of pocket. I learned that your biggest goal is to look as attractive as possible to a lender; this might mean bringing in one or more partners or your own stash of funding. You want to show a lender that you have skin in the game and give them the confidence to back you. This approach certainly worked for me.

IRON BRIDGE LENDING:
WHO ARE THESE HARD-MONEY GUYS ANYWAY?

Iron Bridge Lending was started in 2009 by Gerard and his wife, Sarah. In the dark days of the recession that started after the crash of 2008, they embarked on a wild ride, starting their lending firm as many investors pulled money out of the market. With Gerard's background in investment banking, they encouraged investors/financial groups to join their fund, and as these dollars came together, it grew to what, in 2016 (when we first began to work with them), was a fund of $80 million that they loan out for fix and flip projects all over the United States.

For your first deal, consider a loan with 10 percent down (maybe you split this with a partner), and then consider using credit cards or additional savings to pay for your fix-ups without the lender financing that part of the flip.

HARD-MONEY LOANS AS HANDY TOOLS

A **hard-money loan** for a real estate purchase is secured by real property—the property for which the loan will be used. Many hard-money lenders don't need your credit score. Instead, they base your ability to repay the loan on other factors: the equity you put down or the amount of equity in the home over the discounted purchase price. Additionally, the loans are usually for about six to twelve months, so lenders expect a quick turnaround.

These types of loans became a great tool, particularly in recent years. The hard-money-lending market has emerged since the financial crisis of 2008. Before the Dodd-Frank Wall Street Reform and Consumer Protection Act was passed, banks were not regulated on how they created loans. Banks could offer the primary loan and then a second one on top of it. Consumers wouldn't know this but ultimately paid interest two different times in that instance. Or banks offered "balloon mortgages," in which the interest rates went up after a certain term of the loan. There was a lot of funny business, so the Dodd-Frank reform tightened regulations on banks, which protects the consumer but creates many more regulations they must meet to get funded.

Thus, the hard-money-loan industry grew because of the extensive rules and legal parameters placed on large lenders (think Fannie Mae), banking institutions, and the loan qualification process. Banks make it tougher to get loans and open opportunities for new types of funding, like hard-money loans, now fueling house flippers all over America and even internationally.

> **BANKS MAKE IT TOUGHER TO GET LOANS AND OPEN OPPORTUNITIES FOR NEW TYPES OF FUNDING, LIKE HARD-MONEY LOANS, NOW FUELING HOUSE FLIPPERS ALL OVER AMERICA AND EVEN INTERNATIONALLY.**

It is important to note other types of loans that emerged from Dodd-Frank for your overall knowledge. Kabbage or "credit card sales loans" pay out quickly (within a week), so they offer instant cash, but come at interest rates up to 25 percent APR until the loan gets repaid. This is really predatory lending. You receive $30,000 fast, but then within the following weeks, you may have $50,000 pulled to repay the $30,000.

Payday lenders also exploded with Dodd-Frank regulations on banks. Payday loans are a relatively small amount of money given at a high interest rate. The promise from the borrower is repayment when they receive their next paycheck.

TIPS FOR GETTING APPROVED FOR A HARD-MONEY LOAN

No matter the loan, it all comes down to getting approved. What does that involve?

1. **Location.** A lot relies on the location of the project. If it's too rural, too far away from a major city, the hard-money lender won't want to fund the project. I've had at least five projects located in rural areas that hard-money lenders simply wouldn't touch.

2. **Valuation.** Companies also look at your overall valuation of the project as it pertains to **ARV**, or the "after-repair value"—how much instant equity will you get as soon as you buy the home? If the ARV is too low,

they don't want the project compared to the purchase price. As they say in the flipping business, you *make* your *value* when you buy the asset; you *capture* the *return* on investment when you sell.

3. **Budget.** Your budget is another factor for approval. What will it take to fix up the property? Costs that are more than 30 percent of the resale price typically present a problem. The percent of rehab on our first few flips was about 7 to 15 percent of the total resale price. We spent less than $10,000 fixing up our first flip by doing all the work ourselves. The budget was just under 7 percent of the $155,000 resale price.

4. **Capital.** What's your skin in the game? We liked that Iron Bridge Lending (and there are many lenders out there that will consider this for you too) lent us the funds for our deals with only 10 percent down plus closing costs (many lenders want 20 percent down).

There are several ways to consider a hard-money loan. Let's go over the pros and cons, and then we'll close with a look at the actual numbers I dealt with during my first dealings with Iron Bridge Lending.

HARD FACTS ON HARD-MONEY LOANS

You may see by now that I'm a big fan of hard-money loans, but you need to know everything about them for yourself. There are pros and cons, and then to confuse the matter, some cons can also be pros. Let's dig into all of this with some words of advice along the way.

1. **Know your timing.** Hard loans have expiration dates. Rates can go up, so you must know your timing when you get a hard-money loan. Can you flip that house and get it sold in three to six months? Have your timing set; know your beginning, middle, and end plan.

2. **There will be higher interest.** A pro and con are that you pay higher interest rates, but you can also secure more money than through traditional financing. To estimate your project loan costs, I encourage you to use our pro forma Excel document at thefundingsolutionbook.com.

3. **Great credit is not necessary.** A big pro is that hard-money lenders aren't looking as closely at your credit score, but you do show them what capital you're working with.

4. **Know your numbers.** Do the due diligence, and be thorough with your documentation. Don't get overwhelmed with paperwork during the first deal. Do your homework— the lenders are going to need all of your budget information. Don't let that intimidate you; just come to the table with the numbers, even if they're close estimations.

5. **Again, ignore the stigma.** There seems to be some fear in telling friends and family you're taking out a hard-money loan. They may say you're too ambitious or naive taking out such a high-interest loan or that it's too risky. It's well intended; they don't want you taken advantage of. You won't be at risk if you take the time up front and confirm your numbers are solid, and you can make the investment with enough equity in the house on day one. It can work! Know your numbers, and don't be concerned with what others think—you know there is enough pie at the end!

6. **Be OK with others making their share.** When you become a business owner, you have to be OK with the notion that others will benefit from you: your employees, customers, and vendors, by extension. In

the same way, hard-money lenders make a healthy profit on these loans, but they also take on the borrowers' considerable risk. Don't let the high rate of interest dissuade you from focusing on the end ROI.

When I started with Brad, we formed an LLC together. We split the ownership percentages fifty-fifty, which allowed us to build trust quickly as we did several flips together. I encourage you to focus on the solid returns as you partner with someone on a flip, or even possibly more than one. Don't get greedy thinking of how you could make more doing it solo. You will always accomplish more with others than without them.

THE NUTS AND BOLTS OF THE NUMBERS GAME

Below are our numbers from the first Iron Bridge Lending deal.

We had a choice: Two and 14 percent for six months, or three and 12 percent for twelve months. We paid more on the money for a longer term, but it was at a lower rate.

The "two" or "three" above refer to **percentage points** (called the **origination fee**); they are points on the overall cost of the loan. The 12 and 14 percent are the **APR**, or annual percentage rate. The lender charges the origination fee for processing your application (on a traditional loan, typically .5 to 1.0 percent). The APR is the interest rate you pay over the year to have the loan (the same as a credit card you run a balance on or a car loan).

Brad and I deliberated both options against our project timeline. We felt confident securing the one with lower points and a higher percentage rate. We ran the numbers against the timing and, overall, preferred to pay fewer points on the money. Using a solid pro forma spreadsheet (like the one shared in this chapter) allows you to estimate your points and APR.

WHERE TO FIND A HARD-MONEY LOAN

There are dozens of funds and hard-money lenders nationwide; these are the Big Five:

- RCN Capital

- CoreVest

- Lima One Capital

- Groundfloor

- LendingHome

While these are the nation's largest, I have had much greater success with more regional small-to-medium-sized lenders. Keep in mind, you want (with all of these lenders) to talk to your broker about their fees. Below are just a few things they may charge you. Ask about all of them, as they can add up to anywhere from $3,000 to $7,000, depending on the total loan amount.

Standard fees for a hard-money loan include the following:

- Origination fee: Usually 1 percent to 3 percent

- Broker fee

- Application fee

- Underwriting fee

- Document preparation fee

- Processing fee

- Funding fee

There is a full list of hard-money lenders at the end of the book. You can also find this list with website links on thefundingsolutionbook.com.

At the end of the day, remember not to get stuck on one lender. You have options, including private lenders, which we'll talk about next. Private lenders are looking for experience before they'll consider approving a loan, so it's good to have a project or two under your belt first. I recommend securing a hard-money loan for your first deal or two and then explore what else is out there.

CHAPTER THREE

FINDING DADDY WARBUCKS

IT'S ALL ABOUT PRIVATE LENDING

I'll admit I lived a somewhat sheltered life growing up. My dad was a Christian minister and my mom a nurse. Growing up, I didn't watch

that much television other than some family-favor-
ite movies. I remember my sister Erica and I always
finding the movie *Annie* (the 1982 version) on TV. The
part I latched onto was when Annie came to Oliver
Warbucks's house (played by Albert Finney). Erica
and I were in awe watching Annie, the little redhead
orphan, totally enthralled with her new surroundings:
the mansion, the food, the extravagance, everything!

Whether you've seen the movie or not, you get
the idea! We all need that extra leg up sometimes, or
a *big* leg up in many cases. If you want to succeed on
a scale grander than you can dream, it may be because
of one or several parental figures in your life. One of
the best big picture books on this concept is Robert
Kiyosaki's book *Rich Dad, Poor Dad*.

There are many stories
of parents lifting their kids
on their financial shoulders
and boosting them higher
than they could ever dream.
We all know about Donald
Trump and the legendary story of his father jump-
starting his career. Another story is that of Steve Ells,
the founder of Chipotle.

Ells borrowed $85,000 from his father to start
Chipotle. The first restaurant was a sideline business

raising money to open a fine-dining restaurant (Ells is a Culinary Institute of America graduate). What happened is part of entrepreneur lore, as Chipotle soared as a business and never slowed down. McDonald's invested in the company in 2001. Chipotle went public soon after.

What if you don't have a wealthy parent, uncle, aunt, or multimillionaire to adopt you? What can you do then? Well, I encourage you to find your own Daddy Warbucks. I know it sounds like a crazy idea, but imagine it. If you want to be more successful, imagine having a private lender to lend to you when larger lenders won't. Could more doors be opened? Could you do more profitable deals?

At the signing of our second project, Brad and I got to chatting with our notary; her name was Briana. She asked if we were flippers; it turned out that she and her husband were too. She asked if we needed a lender. We let her know we only used Iron Bridge in Portland. She offered to connect us with her lender, a local private lending group. Briana introduced us, and before we knew it, we had lunch with our new friend and lender, Bob.

We met Bob at a local Mexican joint. He essentially interviewed us, asking lots of questions about our background and projects to date. This was our time to shine. By the time we finished our enchiladas, Bob had offered to start us off with one loan and take it from there. The chance meeting with Briana turned into twenty-plus loans over the next several years from this new-to-us private group—what a delicious enchilada that turned out to be!

So who is Bob? Bob is the lead broker for a private lending group. Private lenders are individuals or a group of individuals (not a company like Iron Bridge) with a line of credit or access to capital that they loan out. In this case, we were lucky enough to meet the individual who managed several families' funds. Bob brokered deals and invested in projects with great potential for his clients.

IT'S CRUCIAL TO HAVE MORE THAN ONE LENDER AT YOUR DISPOSAL; WHAT IF YOUR ONE LENDER SAYS NO? WHAT IF YOU HAD YOUR HEART SET ON THAT PROJECT? WHAT THEN?

More than twenty projects later, finding and securing a private-money lender has been game-changing for us. It's crucial to have more than one lender at your disposal; what if your one lender says no? What if you had your heart set on that project? What then?

The year 2020 brought home the importance of

having multiple lenders. As the world shut down due to a global pandemic, it immediately became challenging to get a loan. Luckily, we had a few lenders we could go to; when one said no, we had another option. These multiple options saved our butts in 2020.

WHERE TO FIND A PRIVATE LENDER

Where do you begin? As you can see, sometimes you simply find yourself in the right place at the right time, but it all boils down to networking. Here are a few ways to network:

1. **Call on real estate agents.** This is another good time to connect with a local real estate agent. As before, they may know local house flippers or even be working with them. It's entirely likely they have an investor or two in their contact list.

2. **Check Craigslist.** No, really. Many private-money guys post their contact information on craigslist, mentioning that they do private-money lending. You never know; it may at least be worth a conversation.

3. **Look for interested friends and family.** Family and friends are more hesitant to open

their wallets at first than anyone else. Approach them once you have proof of your work secured through a hard-money loan. After a project or two, you'll earn their trust in no time.

WHAT HAPPENS DURING A PRIVATE-MONEY LOAN?

Whether it's a hard- or private-money loan, the lender acts as a bank. They put up the resources, and you sign a promissory note and a deed of trust enabling them to serve as the bank on your behalf.

As you look at this alternate means of lending outside of banks, a promissory note provides the legal parameters of the agreement and loan.

WHAT IS A PROMISSORY NOTE?

According to Investopedia.com, a promissory note is: a financial instrument that contains a written promise by one party (the note's issuer or maker) to pay another party (the note's payee) a definite sum of money, either on-demand or at a specified future date. A promissory note typically contains all the terms pertaining to the indebtedness, such as the principal amount, interest rate, maturity date, date and place of issuance, and issuer's signature.

Although financial institutions may issue them, promissory notes are debt instruments that allow companies and individuals to get financing from a source other than a bank.

(Source: Adam Barone, "Promissory Note," Investopedia, accessed September 9, 2021, https://www.investopedia.com/ terms/p/promissorynote.asp#what-is-a-promissory-note.)

THE PROS AND CONS OF PRIVATE LENDING

I love working with private lenders. The primary reason is that you can do more deals with fewer restrictions on the projects (site choice, property condition, and so on). You also avoid fees that bigger lenders incur and require. That said, I want to tell you everything there is to know about getting into a unique relationship such as this. Here's a handy list of what to look out for:

1. **Private lenders are much more relational.** While this is a pro, it can sometimes be a little touchy too. There's a great deal of account-

ability involved in this relationship. The lender isn't necessarily calling you daily; still, they check in a lot more than, say, a hard-money lender because it's their own money. For example, when I have borrowed capital from one of our private lenders, Bruce, he called every other week to check in. More contact can be a good thing, especially for someone getting into their first flip or two; the additional accountability may help you stay focused. In my opinion, this is more a pro than con, but understand there is a lot more oversight and follow-up involved.

2. **More accessible extensions.** Another pro is that there's always a possibility of a loan extension. Hard-money loans are short-term loans, and lenders tend to be laser focused on a deadline. On the other hand, private lenders tend to have much more leniency and grace in extending the loan terms. Suppose it takes longer to finish or sell a house than you had anticipated. In that case, there's significantly more leeway because of the private-money relationship.

3. **Fast-track investment decisions.** The better the private-money relationship, the easier it is to land loans for future projects. For me, this is one of the biggest pros. Once you build a reputation and a track record with an individual or a group, doubt is progressively removed from the relationship. It is then easier to obtain more loans, possibly a lower down payment, or even *no* down payment. Yes, you heard me correctly. Because of our track record, the majority of our loans with Bob require *no* money down. When you can borrow funds with no money down, it can launch you into an even more prosperous future! For example, I recently did what I call the "deal of the decade," which could not have happened without Bob and the trust I've built with him. We found a substantial purchase with a significant upside: one house for sale on a five-acre lot combined with three additional five-acre lots. The three added lots were part of the sale at almost no extra cost. The purchase price was the largest we'd partnered for at $670,000, plus the funds to fix the house up to sell. The three additional lots were bonus revenue opportunities.

4. **Networking:** Private-money loan dealings often result in referrals. Additional projects have come from my private lending relationships. For example, a friend of Bob's needed a flip partner on a foreclosed home he purchased. His original partner had to back out after being diagnosed with cancer. We stepped in and got to work on what turned into a game-changer piece of business for us. As relationships develop into something more personal, you grow closer to their connections and business opportunities.

Finally, **trust payments/owner contracts** are additional options that fall in the vicinity of private lending, but with a twist, which we cover in the next chapter. Whether you're buying a business or a house, owner-financing opportunities are out there—you just have to be on the lookout for them!

CHAPTER FOUR

OWNER CONTRACTS

TACOS AND TRUST PAYMENTS

Best-selling business author and real estate mogul Grant Cardone says it best when he commented that it's a lot easier to raise funds if you de-drama-tize the challenge. In one of his business-focused sessions, Cardone talks about thinking of money as Post-it notes instead of dollars. If you think about raising all these dollars, it can feel overwhelming and intimidating. If you mentally shift them to Post-it notes, they have less meaning, and emotions or negative energy lessen or go away. When you think about it like this, it's a lot easier to get your head around the challenge. Reshaping your mindset to thinking like this can shift your energy. For many people, it's so intimidating to ask others for money or go out and think about receiving a loan for a sizable sum. But if you're honest with yourself, this is exactly what you need: capital (Post-it notes) to be able to fund your project or launch your new business. And if you start thinking in terms of Post-it notes, it's a lot easier to go out and ask for what you need.

Another reason to not feel intimidated about raising a sizable amount for your new business or taking out a loan is the **captured equity** you ultimately obtain with the investment.

Let's use house flipping as an example. When you

buy a house to fix up, you don't make your money on the remodeling, and you don't make it on the sale. The *value* is when you purchase the home at a deeply discounted price—you make the value and then your **equity**. You receive the equity when you sell, but the value is created at the beginning!

Starting a new business is very similar. When you start a business—or, like me, when you buy one—you have the opportunity to generate instant equity. It comes from embarking on a venture that, with sweat equity, will be worth more when you sell than the initial dollars spent to start it.

In 2012 I bought my second franchise, the second Taco Del Mar restaurant we owned and ran in greater Portland, Oregon. The owner, Mr. Miller, also had four Subway sandwich shops, and his wife ran the taco-themed business. I knew he and his wife were at odds about continuing to own it, and he didn't want to have to deal with it anymore. He so desperately wanted to sell that he extended me an offer I couldn't refuse.

Instead of taking out a bank loan or using a private-money source, Mr. Miller offered me his fully operating taco franchise, all the equipment, and even his team for $45,000. It was an incredible steal. I made payments to him for four and a half years at 5 percent interest.

If you know about **owner financing** or had the opportunity to owner finance, you know it can be an incredible tool:

1. It allows the buyer to purchase without as much cash down and buy something when they can't secure a loan. It also allows the buyer to get a lower rate; the purchase at 5 percent is much better than any hard-money lender offers.

2. You are not borrowing from a bank, so your credit score is not affected, and the loan is "off the government books," so to speak. Did you hear that? This is an off-the-books loan, meaning your credit score *is not*—I repeat, *not*—directly affected. If you are in a credit-rebuilding stage, this may be good news for you for that next business opportunity.

But back to the story. The purchase of this Taco Del Mar franchise was pretty exciting because it shows the value of captured equity, along with the owner-financing method's success or utilizing an owner contract.

I encourage you to go onto a website like www.bizbuysell.com if you're interested in buying a business instead of starting one from scratch. In the keyword section, search for businesses that are for sale with "owner financing." These are businesses that, with a moderate amount of money down, you can buy without a bank loan.

When Mr. Miller initially offered to sell his Taco Del Mar restaurant, we agreed to $45,000, with one-third down. But I still believed I was possibly paying too much or that Mr. Miller would sell for less. The day came to sign the final agreement, and I racked my brain for a definitive reason to ask for a deeper discount. Up to this point, each time I visited the business, it was at night, and I always entered the same way. I never noticed a brand-new McDonald's restaurant and drive-through under construction at the far side of the plaza.

I went to sign and meet Mr. Miller so we could close in a week. I pulled into the parking lot and parked. I got out of my green Fiat 500 and saw the banner declaring the grand opening in two weeks. This was also the nicest McDonald's I'd ever seen, with fountains and an arboretum garden out front. I walked into the meeting armed with my ammunition to ask Mr. Miller for a deeper discount.

It went something like this: "Mr. Miller, I'm just a little concerned about this McDonald's about to open in the very front of the plaza. I am not sure I want to move forward with the business purchase. I could buy this business from you and be put out of business in a month because, as we all know, McDonald's is the most popular quick-service restaurant in the world!"

Mr. Miller's face went white, and looking back, I believe this was the reason he was selling. He wasn't as frustrated working with his wife as he was afraid of being annihilated by Mickey D's! What he said next, I've never seen before or since: "Well, Roger, let me do this then. I'll sell it to you for $16,000, and you don't have to put any money down; just pay 5.5 percent." I couldn't believe my ears. Not only did he drop the price by nearly $30,000, but he also didn't require any funds down (the only money I had to come up with was to buy the store inventory for about $5,600).

PURCHASE PRICE
$45,000

NEW PRICE
$16,000

My wife and I ran the franchise for the next four years. At the beginning of year five, we sold for $76,000, almost five times our purchase price.

I share this story to show that business owners will finance you because they are seriously hungry, even desperate, to sell. Additionally, because they own their business outright and have 100 percent equity in their own business, they can act as the bank and finance you. There is another lesson of instant equity: when a business owner is retiring or transitioning, there is a loss or lack of serious, ongoing interest. This is *your gain.*

I have one more story to illustrate this point.

Stacey and I were hit hard during the 2008 recession, along with many others. As housing prices fell, we short-sold our home in 2011 at close to a $100,000 loss. We rented for a year before moving north to the Greater Tacoma area of Washington state. When we moved, we were still in a two-year waiting period before buying another house because of the short-sale rules of the banking and mortgage industry. We remained focused on grabbing an opportunity to buy again, now in a down market. We found it with a family friend looking to sell. It just so happened they had 100 percent equity in their home; they owned it outright. I think you know where this is going.

This situation is scarce. Because the majority of US homes have mortgages, owner financing is not possible. We made a deal with our friend Sheila and her mom, Grandma Ordy. We bought their house for $282,000, putting $13,500 in cash down at the signing. They then financed us two years. Their goal was to help us and ensure we'd refinance and pay her off in exactly two years. To ensure this, she increased the interest from 5 percent in the first twenty-four months to 8.5 percent starting at the twenty-fifth month. This provided our motivation to get her paid off very quickly.

It worked like clockwork; after two years, we passed the waiting period and got the refinance through a lender. On the July Fourth weekend in 2013, we paid Grandma Ordy and moved into the home of our dreams. We still live in that home today!

When we went to sign the papers, the title representative was shocked at the arrangement: "I don't think I've ever seen a deal like this before; this is highly unusual. Mrs. O. is

YES, THAT IS PRECISELY WHAT OWNER CONTRACTS ON A PROPERTY ARE AND HOW THEY GET SET UP; THE EQUITY IN A PROPERTY OWNED OUTRIGHT ALLOWS THE SELLER TO ACT AS THE BANK.

acting as the bank!" Yes, that is precisely what owner contracts on a property are and how they get set up; the equity in a property owned outright allows the seller to act as the bank.

When you identify an investment property, a flip, or investment rental, remember you can ask the seller to make an owner contract. You just want to keep in mind that they will expect payment in the short term. Here are a couple of items to consider with an owner contract:

1. A larger down payment. (This may be necessary to convince the seller to do an "owner carry.")

2. A higher interest rate. (The seller may carry the property if they know they are getting a higher interest rate for one to two years before being paid off in full.)

3. Personal guarantee. (They most likely will ask you to sign a personal guarantee. This means you can't put the property into an LLC and not be 100 percent personally liable for the loan. They are acting like the bank, so they want to be sure they get paid off.)

4. An amortization schedule (twenty-five to thirty years) that favors the amount of interest the seller will receive per month.

You can be as creative as you want to be with owner contracts; it often comes down to how much the seller wants to sell their property and how much they like you and want to help you as you detail your need for "creative lending" and a "unique loan solution."

As you think through and create your offer for a seller, I recommend running and including amortization schedules. These allow you to calculate how your monthly payments break down between the interest and principal (paying down the loan itself). It's pretty simple: visit bankrate.com or mortgage.calc.com to create them using the loan amount, interest rate, and term.

Here is the breakdown for our schedule: Grandma Ordy loaned us $282,000 *minus* $13,500 = $268,500. This number goes into the mortgage calculator, and I run an amortization schedule at 5 percent. You can run this through the calculator to see what we paid: a $1,585.11 monthly payment, and $1,122.61 was the interest. When you add up how much Grandma Ordy received, she made 5 percent on her money. While this is not great, it is not horrible either, and we got fairly good financing for the term we needed.

As you approach a seller, keep in mind that the amount of interest you offer and how you create your amortization schedule is the key to convincing the seller to go with your proposal.

While it may be challenging to find this kind of opportunity, you may even use this owner contract arrangement with a family member with a home they'd sell you. Don't be afraid to approach different situations with the owner contract arrangements, as it allows you to sidestep traditional bank lending and find a solution that works for you!

I hope these few stories show the value of pursuing and learning about owner financing. I had the privilege of purchasing two other businesses, empty lots, and other properties on owner contracts. It is a great way to leverage debt and not be held down by your credit score while generating trust between two individuals doing business together.

At the root of it, this may be hard to wrap your mind around; literally, hundreds of thousands of individuals every day enter into good-faith loan-repayment plans between one another without the banks. No banks. I repeat, lending without needing bank approval, only seller and buyer approval. Doesn't that sound liberating—even jaw dropping?

If you're like me, you've had many hurdles and disappointments with bank lending and a bank or lender saying no. It's time to try asking a seller for an owner-financing opportunity.

In any lending situation, things can go wrong. In our next chapter, we'll talk about what to look for when you take that leap of faith to start your own business or get into house flipping.

CHAPTER FIVE

PARTNERSHIPS

DON'T BE AFRAID TO SHARE THE LOAD AND GAIN

Remember *The Lord of the Rings* books and film trilogy? Frodo Baggins and Samwise Gamgee's relationship provides a similar model for house flips and short-term investment partnerships. The ring was always Frodo's load to bear, but Samwise supported Frodo every step of the way. In your investments, your role may be Frodo's: to lead and initiate. When you know the challenges to come, having a Samwise by your side is a good idea. "Share the load," as they say. You may find a partner at the end of the journey that helps carry you to finish the race.

TO GO 50/50 OR TO NOT GO 50/50?

When you're going into a partnership around real estate transactions, I believe it's best to split the share and responsibilities down the middle, 50/50. I don't necessarily believe in this as a business ownership partnership model; those are long term and more complicated. With house flips, if you and a partner split the responsibility to complete the project (trips to the property, phone calls to subcontractors, and other necessary day-to-day tasks), unless you do the majority of work yourself or have a silent partner, it's OK to go 50/50. In my opinion, projects go better when partners split everything, especially when it's a side project and not your full-time job. It's good for morale. If one partner is doing more work but doesn't have an equal share, or vice versa, they may feel disdain for the project if they worry about fair compensation.

That said, if I find the property and have more responsibility, I don't split the deal 50/50. Once I turned this into a business, unequal splits happen more often. I now manage more of the behind-the-scenes work on a project. The key to an unequal division is clearly laying out each person's role.

SPLITTING UP SHARES

I set up an unequal share partnership with my friend Mike for a Lincoln City project on the Oregon Coast. The split was 75/25, with me taking a 75 percent share. Why? When we created the partnership, we confirmed that I would take on the lion's share of responsibility to complete the flip. I would show up more. I lined up the lending and talked to the Realtors. I was 100 percent responsible for all of the fix-up costs, including labor and materials. Mike was to help work on the house, painting, inside touch-ups, a little carpentry, and meeting with subcontractors, including roofers and the electrician. Mike paid the majority of the down payments, about $55,000. Mike contributing the equity was the main reason I partnered with him. We then split the loan payment 75/25.

The project went a bit long, with challenges com-

WE BOTH WALKED AWAY HAPPY CAMPERS—ALL BECAUSE, FROM THE GET-GO, WE CLEARLY DEFINED OUR ROLES.

pleting the roof due to weather. But we finished the flip and sale in eight months, making $46,900. Mike took 25 percent, and we both walked away happy campers—all because, from the get-go, we clearly defined our roles. Mike was a great partner.

THREE PARTNERSHIP PARTICULARS

After years of forming numerous partnerships, I identified three things to consider when forming them.

1. **Roles.** What are the roles in the partnership? Who's doing what?

2. **Money.** Who's bringing what equity to the investment? Who's bringing what dollar amount to the initial purchase? Who is paying for the fix-up? Are those split 50/50?

3. **Loan.** Who is paying for the loan payments?

Once you know these particulars, put every detail into a promissory note.

PROMISSORY NOTES: PARTNERING LEGALLY

Before closing on the new project, Mike and I wrote a promissory note confirming that my company owned 100 percent of the property but Mike was entitled to 25 percent of the profit on the resale for his loan amount.

When it comes to closing, you may form partnerships in one of two ways: form an LLC or sign a promissory note.

LLC. You can choose for both partners to be on the title, meaning you both buy the property together as well as forming an LLC together.

Promissory note. I mentioned promissory notes previously with private lending, and they apply here as well. If you have equity and bring in a partner, you will buy the project yourself and include a promissory note outlining how much project ownership the partner has.

There are two kinds of promissory notes: secured and nonsecured. A family member, friend, or a close business relation may write a nonsecured note; a nonsecured note is in good faith that you will pay it back. Secured promissory notes must state that the borrowed dollars be secured by the asset the money is loaned for or identify another asset.

Promissory notes will almost always be secured by the property, making them a very straightforward way to bring in potential investors for your project.

Here's something to understand about a secured promissory note: if it's secured by the property you're investing in, and you don't add the lender on the title, they can use it to "lien the property" for the loaned amount of money if you do not pay them back. This means they can take the promissory note to their attorney or a title or escrow office to file documentation stating that they are owed the amount on the promissory note upon sale of the property.

Much like travel, flipping houses brings a new experience around every other corner, which will only help you (and the amount of money in your bank account) grow.

What do you do if you buy a foreclosed home sight unseen only to find a caved-in roof and pools of rainwater everywhere? Let me tell you all about what I did in chapter 6.

CHAPTER SIX

TWISTS AND TURNS

WHEN TO PIVOT

During our second year of flipping, my partner and I worked on a project in Gig Harbor, Washington. This particular project turned into a pretty big headache, as the scope kept growing and growing. Dollars kept going out the door with remodeling and renovations. We unexpectedly replaced the roof and identified numerous electrical upgrades. One challenge came after another, and $30,000 later, we found ourselves pretty far over budget.

− $30,000

Thankfully, we rarely find ourselves in this predicament, but challenges do come up. I accepted years ago with this overbudget flip that sometimes we have to pivot. It was a lesson I learned again when the coronavirus pandemic hit, and lenders stopped lending.

What do you do when that happens? Breathe and think things through clearly. Take the time, if you can, and talk to your partner about all possible smart solutions. Accept that you may take a hit here or there, but the eventual reward makes it all worth it. That's precisely what happened with the Gig Harbor project.

WHAT COULD GO WRONG?

GOING OVER BUDGET

So what did we do about being enormously over budget? First, we spoke to Bob, our lender, and asked him to consider extending our repayment deadline. We trusted that Bob knew our work and that we would complete the project. We exhaled a huge sigh of relief when he agreed. However, he would not provide more funds, so we had to find additional capital, around $30,000. Luckily, our credit cards had additional lines of credit that we used for business purposes only. Before now, we began varying our options in case of an emergency, so we had a lifeline (or three). We stretched ourselves thin with credit cards, the loan extension, and a home equity loan to finish. We also brought in extra expertise to support project completion. We sold it at a loss, but a smaller one than if we had not made the right "pivot."

Sometimes you just have to pivot! Here are a few more scenarios to look out for:

GROWING PAINS WITH HARD-MONEY LENDERS

We worked with another great partner and large lender, Sound Equity (now Sound Capital). From the outset, we brought them nothing but slam-dunk deals; this set us on a great path, earning their trust and, subsequently, their dollars. If you have a hard time getting a lending deal, try to find a deal that makes financial sense, from the purchase price to the rehab budget. Once we earned their trust with our first solid deal, Sound Equity was eager to lend to us with zero hesitation. Once we had a few projects under our belts, we excelled at securing great deals (like half-off deals) on properties because they were a little out of the way. I am now comfortable searching for deals out of state, flipped properties on islands, and locations three hours away from my home. That progression was only possible due to my great, growing relationship with a large lender.

> IF YOU HAVE A HARD TIME GETTING A LENDING DEAL, TRY TO FIND A DEAL THAT MAKES FINANCIAL SENSE, FROM THE PURCHASE PRICE TO THE REHAB BUDGET.

GETTING APPRAISALS

The biggest drawback is getting a hard-money lender to sign off on a house in a remote place. To secure one, in some cases, they want to order a full appraisal, which can be $800 to $1,200. You have to pay for this in good faith, not knowing if the lender will go through with the deal or not, but if it's a good enough deal, it's worth the risk.

In many cases, a hard-money lender may do their own assessment of the property or an internal broker price opinion (**BPO**). Frequently, when reviewing the house value, they decide there's not enough equity in the deal to move forward with a loan. In that case, ordering an independent appraisal may be worth the expense if the margins are good enough.

We had deals valued at $60 to $70 per square foot that, once fixed up, would be worth $250 per square foot. These would not get funded without pushing the lender a little and getting our own appraisals. If you think you have a solid bet, do what you have to do to fund it!

EXTRA ORIGINATION FEE POINTS

In some situations, the lender may want an extra point to point and a half more on the loan's origination fee. This may happen if they deem a project riskier or out of the way, or if they believe the ARV (after-repair value) is not high enough based on their metrics. It's definitely a tricky situation to prepare for.

With that Gig Harbor home, we were in deep and could not panic about being over budget; we had to be rational and figure out the best next steps to keep moving forward. In the end, this project became a great memory. We worked through the funding steps and brought in the support we needed to complete the flip. A bonus was that it became a family affair. Several family members put in a lot of the work instrumental to a positive outcome. Rich

Myers, my rock-star brother-in-law, and my mother-in-law, Vicki, were working the day the future owners stopped by. As folks painted and put on the finishing touches, they talked up the house to the interested couple and completely sold them.

OTHER TWISTS AND TURNS

Twists and turns are part of the deal, but never fear—there's *always* a solution. You just have to be resourceful.

Here are a couple of examples of times we had to think on our feet and *outside* the box!

EASTER EGG SURPRISE: OUR FIRST WHOLESALE DEAL

You cannot always get inside foreclosures before you close, so you never know what you're going to get! It's like a box of chocolates.

The following illustrates a time there was enough equity in the deal that the lender was all in. Still, for us, the flippers, plenty of surprises lay in store.

My last Iron Bridge Lending loan was for a house near my sister, Erica, in Pittsburgh, Pennsylvania. We thought it'd be fun to collaborate on a few basic projects while I visited her. We started one that was going great when we saw a second property for sale. It was in a great neighborhood and in foreclosure, selling for about $112,000. We felt strongly that once fixed up, it could be worth $300,000 to $400,000. The only challenge was that we couldn't get into the property! The window shades were all drawn, and we couldn't even get a peek. The location was phenomenal, so we committed to it. When the lender saw the equity, they were in too—without an appraisal or an internal BPO.

I called this property the Easter egg because we had no idea what we would find when we opened the door. I arrived in Pittsburgh, and we drove to the house the following day. We knocked on the door, but no one answered. Walking around the house, we found the back door open, so we walked in. It was like nothing I've seen in my career. To date, I had completed fifty or so projects but never had experienced something this intense. We entered and found all of their belongings and more. Things were everywhere: mountains of trash bags and boxes stacked to the ceiling, a rotting deck in the back connected to a neglected aboveground pool.

Everything had to go.

Oh, and there was a third floor with its roof completely caved in. If you know anything about

Pittsburgh, you know the rain there is much like in the Pacific Northwest. There were pools of water throughout the house from this large, gaping hole in the roof. The owners had tried collecting the rain with multiple huge plastic bins. It was a mess.

At this point, any flipper would be completely flummoxed; I collected myself and processed the information before me. I knew one thing to be true: this flip would be very involved. I knew it required support to flip it all the way and decided to treat this one a little differently. In the flipping business, there are wholesale deals in which you act as the go-between. Traditionally, this means that you buy and sell without even flipping it. You do not make upgrades, updates, or renovations of any kind. You buy it at one price to turn around and sell for a little bit more.

And that is what we did. We ultimately replaced the roof, got rid of the deck and pool, cleared the trash out, and cleaned the house from top to bottom. I got a permit for a dumpster, and I hired a crew to remove everything. We filled four sixty-foot-long dumpsters for a total of $11,000. We replaced the roof for $7,000. We spent $18,000 in total to be ready to sell. Three weeks later, we listed it for $165,000 and sold it for $160,000, making a cool $34,711.46 at closing without even completing the flip. It wasn't what we initially envisioned, but we were happy with how we handled it and the profit we walked away with.

CHICAGO TITLE		8741

8741

CHICAGO TITLE   20____

PAY TO THE ORDER OF *Roger Becker* $ | 34,711.46 |

Thirty-Four Thousand Seven Hundred Eleven & ⁶⁵/₁₀₀ DOLLARS

BANK OF THE WORLD

MEMO _____   *Roger Becker*

⑈1234567890⑈ ⑆67890⑆ ⑈8741⑈

A flip can be overwhelming. That's a lesson we all learn time and again. You learn to stop, breathe, and take time to assess the situation and identify how to move forward in ways that make the most sense for you.

When it seems like a dead end, remember it's OK to pivot. You must ask yourself, *What's the win-win here?* I lived in another state and knew what this flip needed. I couldn't commit to the time in Pittsburgh it required. So the win-win was to make a little cash and move on, leaving the place in good enough shape for another flipper to move right into the transformation process.

CONCLUSION

PERSISTENCE

VISUALIZE, EXECUTE, AND KEEP BUILDING

If you have not secured a hard-money loan, the most significant first deal roadblock may be that you cannot imagine your future success. You have to vision cast it! If you don't envision finding a good deal or investment or don't believe you can figure it out, your dreams may never come true. Visualization can change everything!

Imagine it all...think about reaching out and making that first call on a property. Take two more steps; you partnered with a friend for this first project. Now visualize obtaining your first hard-money loan. Boom—you secured your first property.

Picture walking into *your* first flip, envisioning all the promise before you, all the things you and your team can do. Imagine the milestones, the finished hardwood floors, polished banister, shiny new kitchen appliances, tiles and countertops, the landscaping, and even the new mailbox. Imagine walking away from your completed project. You are proud of your work; you forged new relationships and identified partners for your next flip.

HOW WILL YOU SPEND THIS MONEY? A VACATION? YOUR NEXT FLIP? PAYING OFF LOANS OR SAVING FOR YOUR CHILD'S COLLEGE TUITION? THE POSSIBILITIES ARE ENDLESS.

The final step is the closing, and you receive your $25,000 profit check! Wow, how would that feel?

Keep going. Imagine two more completed flips in your second year, one for a $30,000 profit and the next a $40,000 profit. How will you spend this money? A vacation? Your next flip? Paying off loans or saving for your child's college tuition? The possibilities are endless.

Three years in, you have much more experience and confidence; you go after and accomplish three projects. These three projects earn you $35,000, $40,000, and $75,000.

Envision all your success in your first three years. How would making this kind of money change your life or your family's future? Would you have a different outlook on your career? Would you stay with your job or step away to start investing full-time?

If you can imagine realizing this outcome in years one, two, and three, how does your confidence change about finding your first lender?

WHERE DO WE GO FROM HERE?

You visualized your future: finding your partner, securing a loan, and identifying the right project. You've read this book and have the tools you need. So what's your first step?

1. INTERVIEW THREE LENDERS

Please do me a favor. Will you do that? Commit to reaching out to three lenders. Don't wait until you have a project lined up to start making the calls to find a lender. When you call, ask these key questions:

- What are their approval criteria? Do they require a specific credit score?

- What kind of down payment do they require? What percentage of the loan amount?

- Will they roll the closing costs into the loan, or do you have to bring that in as an investment on the first deal?

- How much time does the lender need to close when you apply to sign the finalized loan?

2. IDENTIFY A PARTNER

After you ask the above questions, you'll know what you're working with. You will see if you need to recruit someone to do the project with you, helping bring in the money to secure the investment. That's how I did my first deal—I couldn't have done it (or many after that) without a partner.

Your next action step: Decide whether you need a partner and whether that person should be a spouse, friend, family member, or friend of a friend. Remember, this is a short-term business relationship; you can decide later if this partnership was beneficial enough to keep or if you'd instead let it be!

3. RESEARCH PROPERTIES

Now it's time to get out there and find the perfect deal. For the first investment, remember that it's a good idea to get something close to home, not far from where you live and work, and confirm that the margins look good. The better the profits, the happier the lender, which improves the odds of getting future projects approved!

* * *

A few short years ago, I stood in a gross fourplex unit, envisioning past the stained carpets and the disgusting stench and straight to the future I was about to build, one fresh coat of paint at a time. With good lending advice from a friend, I was on my way, grateful I could move past my hesitation and plan a better tomorrow for my family. Today, I've flipped and invested many times over and am still building and hooked on discovering what's behind the next door.

The time is now. Roll up your sleeves, get out there, and change your future *now*!

PRIVATE / HARD MONEY LENDER LIST

Express Capital Financing
https://www.expresscapitalfinancing.com

Lima One Capital
https://limaone.com

Genesis Capital
https://genesiscapital.com/

Corevest Finance
https://www.corevestfinance.com

Civic Financial Services
https://www.civicfs.com

Gorilla Capital
https://gorillacapital.com

Iron Bridge Lending
https://ironbridgelending.com

Lending Home
https://www.lendinghome.com

Patch of Land
https://patchofland.com

RCN Capital
https://rcncapital.com

Visio Lending
https://www.visiolending.com

Stratton Equities
https://www.strattonequities.com/

Anchor Loans
https://www.anchorloans.com/

Arkad Capital
http://www.thearkadgroup.com

Groundfloor
https://groundfloor.us

Lending One
https://lendingone.com

Residential Capital Partners
https://residentialcapitalpartners.com

Finance of America
https://www.financeofamerica.com

Printed in the USA
CPSIA information can be obtained
at www.ICGtesting.com
JSHW072028140824
68134JS00044B/3837